Single Moms Rock!

How to Survive and Thrive as a Single Mom

Kei Renae

Printed in the United States of America

Book Cover design by ShoreFast Printing

ISBN:0615972284
ISBN-13:9780615972282

SINGLE
MOMS
ROCK

DEDICATION

This book is dedicated to my two children Kevin and
Danae; for without you I would not possess the drive that
I have.
I love you both more than you could ever imagine. This is
all for you.

"For everyone to whom much is given, from him much will be required…….."- Luke 12:48 (NKJV)

Yes this is me at a very young age

CONTENTS

ACKNOWLEDGMENTS

There are so many people I would like to thank. So many people who helped mold me into the woman I am today. So let's begin:

I would like again to thank my son Kevin and daughter Danae for helping me have a purpose in life.

I want to thank my Mom and Dad for giving me life and always having my back! For without you this could never be possible.

My stepfather Richard for being there when my father could not.

My best friend Tiffany Burrell, I have known you since kindergarten and I love you like a sister.

My sisters Tina and Sherron (RIP), Michelle and brother Punchy. We had so much fun growing up and the best childhood any child could ever wish for! Oh, the innocence of those days!

Arlicia "AC" Chrestotholos, my sister from another mother for ALWAYS having my back! The shennigans we used to pull; legendary!

My mentor Mrs. A for helping me keep a level head and providing guidance over the years. Thank you for treating me like your 4th daughter!

Quiche Jones – "the voice of reason", for always lending a non-judgmental ear.

My cousin Doreatha Boynton for always accepting me into my father's side of the family.

For my high school guidance counselor who would constantly tell me that I was an underachiever and she was so right!

My cousin Daytonia Singleton for always speaking your mind and serving as my sounding board for many years.

Dana Reeves for always believing in me and providing support for me to finish college.

Linda Whittaker, wherever you are out there, for serving as my shoulder to cry on for many years.

My "Aunt V", Verona Lester, for watching me grow up and always being there for the important events.

Christopher Williams for showing me how a real man treats a lady. I am so grateful that you have come into my life.

Aunt Kathy, Nancy and Manny for always being an active part in my and Kevin's life.

Rozlyn Carter for being that down 'behind' chick that I can always call and talk to despite what is going on in your life.

Thanks to Alesha Williams Boyd for serving as editor of this book. If you ever run out of 'gas' again I got you!

To my Guardian Angels, my grandmother Gloria Rhoden and great-grandparents Lillian and Leopold Rhoden. I know you are watching over me in heaven. I can't wait to meet you in the next lifetime!

I sincerely hope I did not forget anyone. If I have forgotten any one please forgive me as it is not on purpose; you know my heart.

Lastly I want to thank those who deceived me, wronged me, hated on me, cheated me, tried to defame my character or lied to me or on me. Because of you I have become a better person and you have helped shaped my character into the woman I am today. This Bud's for you (smile).

"If you can't be content with what you have received, be thankful for what you have escaped" – Author unknown

CHAPTER 1
ATTITUDE DETERMINES ALTITUDE

Hi! Meet Kei Renae. I might be considered another statistic by society had I not made a conscious decision that I wouldn't be one. I am a young, single, African-American mother with two kids who beat the odds. I make a very good living. I became a homeowner by the age of 30. I finished college and pride myself in having an MBA with a concentration in general management. It took me about ten years to finish college part-time but most important, I did it!

By no means was it an easy task and I thought about giving up many times. I made mistakes along the way, but again, the important part is that I did it. And you can, too. I am living proof that with the right will, determination, and attitude it can be done. You can make a better life for yourself and your children.

Those times when I wanted to give up, I wondered what would become of my children and I. I held on and persevered. There were things that I did to support my family that I was not proud of, like selling jewelry at the local pawn shop, borrowing money from family that I had no intention of paying back and even dating men purposely for financial support. I did what I had to do in order to provide for my family as necessary. All that I can say is that God has walked with me along this journey. I am by no means a holy roller, nor do I claim to know the Bible back and forth, but I know that I love God and that is all that is important.

As a single mother I can tell you that it has been a long, hard and arduous journey. When I grew weary a little voice inside told me to keep going, and keep going. I would keep going until the next doubtful episode.

Please understand this. Not everyone is going to be in your corner routing for you. There is several reasons that this may occur. The first that comes to mind is jealousy. Yes people that you may think are down for you may actually be jealous of you. Now, don't go around thinking that everyone is hating on you. I'm not saying that everyone that is not in your corner is a so called 'hater'. I'm sorry to tell you this but sometimes this is true; everyone is not always out to get you.

Another reason may be that people tend to be afraid of and avoid uncertainty. People avoid change like the plague and may be scared for you to change your life. We can sit here all night and try to guess the reasons why family and friends may not be in your corner as you recreate your life. The fact is that it does happen and you should be prepared in the event that it happens in your life.

I had people in my own life tell me that I needed to stop attending school and get on welfare or get a full time job to take care of my son. If I listened to everyone that told me to stop, that I shouldn't go to school, that it was never the right time, I would not be where I am today. There will never be a right time for anything. If you keep making excuses and putting things off, the next day will become the next year, then the next three years and so on and so forth. You will awake one day and wonder where the last five years of your life escaped to. You will wonder why you had not taken steps sooner to correct this long path of doom that you have been on. You will realize that you had been going in circles instead of setting measurable goals and progressing toward a brighter future. You are experiencing insanity!

What is the definition of insanity? It is doing the same thing over and over and expecting different results. I personally was tired of getting the same result year after year! Ask yourself, are you tired of experiencing the same thing in your life year after year? If you answered 'yes' to this question then today is the first day of the rest of your life. It is time for you to do something about that.

In terms of my own life there was a flame that always burned inside of me that just would not let me give up. So, every once in a while I would switch my routine up and try a different path. When you feel yourself getting lazy, take a break for a few days to recharge but then rev back up and get ready to continue on your journey. If door A did not work for you, go back and try Doors B, C or X!

I have always been one to be a risk-taker, one who lives life on the edge. I am the one to go where no one else goes. New experiences excite me. I have a thirst to learn new things and I think that is what keeps me going. I could never take anything for face value. If someone says the sky is blue, I want to look behind the clouds to find out why. It is natural for a person to ask questions. You should do your research or inquire about things that do not sit right with you.

I remember that when I had my first born I was on welfare for a few months. While it was very nice to stay home with my little bow-boo-ski, at some point the small stipend that welfare was providing was just not enough to get us through the month. I knew that I had to do something a little better than sitting home and collecting a check each month. I needed a job that was flexible and that would allow me have enough time with my new baby and not make me feel like I was neglecting him.

I decided to go into home health care. I took a two week course and became a certified home health aide. It was not the most glorious of jobs but it was flexible and paid the bills for the time being. I worked in nursing homes, private homes, washed bodies, cleaned kitchens, and changed elderly folk's diapers. You name it. Anything and everything involved in taking care of the elderly; I did it. It was not a fabulous job but hey, you do what you have to do in order to take care of your loved ones. I would eventually move up the career ladder as I will explain later in this book but the point is that many times you have to start at the bottom and work your way up. As I think back I would not have it any other way. When everything is not handed to you on a silver platter and you have to earn it you appreciate it more.

Let me say first off: I am by no means a psychologist, counselor or psychiatrist. But what I am is a self-proclaimed expert on gaining success as a single mother. I experienced it and can tell you what I have learned and what I know from my experiences and the knowledge I have gained along the long journey to where I am today.

Many times people seek out advice from people who have never had experience with certain situations. Well, that can help you to a certain extent – the people can tell you what they think they know, or what happened to someone they know, but they cannot tell you first hand that they actually know.

Stop getting advice from people who have never experienced a situation. Would you get advice from your physician regarding the laws on child support in your state? No.

Would you get marriage advice from a girlfriend who has never married? No. Sure, your girlfriend can tell you what she heard or what happened to a married friend of hers, but she cannot give you firsthand advice regarding marriage. Second hand advice is like the telephone game, once the story reaches you it is more watered down than a glass of Kool-Aid. (More important, you should not be asking a girlfriend for advice on your marriage – you should be talking to your spouse; but that's another book for another time.)

Advice is advice. You can take it or leave it. But who better to get advice from than a person who has lived through what you're going through and survived it, even become successful during the experience? My situation may be different from yours but I am sure there are some similarities. If you are a single mother that is struggling in life, if you've been knocked down several times, I have been there, too. I'm just like you!

I am here to tell you that I was a single parent at the age of 18 and 21 years later I am still standing. I have a Master of Business Administration, two beautiful children, I became a homeowner at the age of 30 and let's just say I earn a pretty good salary in my current careerh9. I think I did darn good if I may say so myself. Yes, I am tooting my own horn!

I can tell you firsthand that what does not kill you makes you stronger and let's just say I am not dead!
If you want to know how I did it, keep reading. You too can survive and thrive as a single mother!

As we become older there are things in life that start to matter less. Most important on the roster is leading a happy and healthy life – making sure your health is OK, your kids and their health are OK. If you are not in decent health mentally and physically then you will not be able to function to your full capacity. We need you at 100 %!

It is also important that you are set for the future financially and that you have decent credit. In this day, good credit says so much about a person like painting a picture about the type of person that you may be, whether you have participated in criminal activity, whether you pay your bills on time and so forth. Timely bill payments shows responsibility and also indicates that you care about your reputation enough that to make sure your credit is in order. My last employer actually performed a credit check on me as a stipulation of my job placement. At first I could not understand this but I now see the purpose of checking the background of future employees.

If you are currently employed and you are in a dead in job, make a plan to find a job that you love. Make sure you are doing what you want in your career and you can make yourself happy. Remember, if you cannot be happy with yourself first, you cannot depend on someone else to make you happy. There is nothing more gratifying than determining what your true calling is on this earth, finding out the reason that God put you here.

I have always wondered what my purpose was on this earth and I think I may have found it. I was put here to tell my story and to encourage other single parents to do the same.

If I can touch even one person and share what I have learned then perhaps I can make another woman's journey easier. Perhaps I can prevent another woman from taking the dead-end streets that I took. Always shoot for the moon – even if you miss you will land among the stars, as the saying goes.

You also gain a new appreciation for life as you get older. The things that used to matter don't matter anymore. Don't put your energy into negative things and people. Instead, always surround yourself with positive things and people! Being negative always takes so much more energy than being positive. Don't get caught in that trap. Sadly enough you will find that some people literally cannot function unless their life is full of negativity and drama. Don't be one of those people. Stay clear of the drama. You will be a better person for it.

At times I ask myself: Why am I so blessed? Then I think: Why not me? I deserve it, right? I have gone through plenty of struggle and strife to arrive at the point that I am at today. I never gave up hope for greener pastures because I knew with hard work I would succeed. There were many times I did not even know where my next meal was coming from. I would spend my last money making sure that my son had lunch and I would eat Chef Boyardee out of a can or I would go to sleep in my car during work so that I would not think about food. I didn't live in the best areas and sometimes even lived with other people because I could not keep a roof over the head of myself and my child.

As the years went on, though, things would take a turn and eventually there was a light at the end of the tunnel. I walked toward the tunnel and never looked back. What I am about to say is a cliché, but it's true: Life is too short.

One day my coworker asked me if I noticed on my commute how pretty the leaves looked. I told her I really had not noticed but promised to make it a point to take a look at the leaves on my way home from work.

Prior to this time, I would always take time to appreciate the small things, including the beauty of nature. What had happened that I had become too busy to stop and admire the little things? When had my life become such a rush that I did not have time to breathe in the fresh autumn air and admire the colorful foliage with which Mother Nature had blessed us?

It was definitely time for a pause. And that is exactly what I did – took a deep breath and promised myself to take my time in life.

Taking the time to appreciate the small things in life allows you to better appreciate life. Life is so precious and valuable that there is no price tag that can be placed on it. I have seen people live a short life and never take the time to appreciate their surroundings.

Have you ever walked amongst a flower garden and just admired the vivid colors of the roses, lilies, or tulips? Have you ever knelt down and ran your fingers gently over the petals; all the while inhaling the tantalizing aroma of one of Mother Nature's best gifts to the world? If not, what better time to start than today?

Here are some things that I do on occasion to bring me back to the simplicity when my life gets hectic:

After putting the children to bed, I took time to myself to unwind by watching a movie or documentary on television. If this is not for you, some other suggestions may be to crotchet a scarf, read a book of poems, try your hand at painting; these are just a few options. Perhaps a glass of wine, a cup of tea, or bowl of popcorn goes well with these ideas as well!

While alone at home, I would sometimes get a pillow and a blanket and practice my own form of meditation. If you are interested, try by first sitting against the wall on top of the pillow and drape the blanket around yourself or on your lap so that you feel comfortable.

Take deep breaths slowly in and out for about 5 minutes. Relax your body and mind and let all the toxins leave your body. This is an exercise I used to do almost every day during the time I was laid off from work. It is a very mild form of meditation. There are many ways to meditate but find one that you are more comfortable with. If you really want to get jiggy with it; there are several

DVDs and CDs on the market that will provide you with in-depth instruction on meditation techniques.

One of my other favorite things to do in warm weather was take a walk on the beach or park and carry a journal with me to record my thoughts or make a list of goals I needed to accomplish for the week. Writing or journaling is a great way of getting all your thoughts out of your mind and on paper. Let's face it, this old brain of mine only benefits from me writing down ideas and thoughts that I can always go back and revisit! If I write it down as I think of it, it's a win-win situation all around!

Try something not listed here. Do something creative that you've never done like parasailing. I tried parasailing for the first time during a last minute trip to Miami Beach in 2012 with a group of wonderful friends! It is an experience like no other and a fantastic way to relax. When parasailing you are thousands of feet in the air and you are one with the elements! Try it, trust me on this one!

Negative Nellie

In the past, when my son was very young, there was a period in my life in which I was always a negative person! I was a Debbie Downer; a gloom and doom type of person. At that time in my eyes, whatever could go wrong would absolutely, positively go wrong every time! The funny thing about this is that I did not even realize the extent of my negativity until a boyfriend brought it to my attention. I told him that he was wrong and caught an attitude. Then I experimented and I listened to myself talk. He was totally right! I decided to work on my constant negativity. From then on out I decided to change my way of my thinking. My thinking has since changed for the better when I decided that I only wanted positive energy around me.

The positive energy that you put in the universe will come back to you tenfold. I am a firm believer in that philosophy. So just try and be a positive person in all that you do. In some situations this will be difficult and with some interactions with negative folks this will be even more difficult.

Once I had gotten past that Negative Nellie Phase, I can recall a run-in that I had with a supposed "hater." I had been hearing whispers that she did not care for me. I was confused about these whispers because to my knowledge I had never done her wrong. One night, while she and I were both at a birthday party for a mutual friend. We were standing about 5 paces from one another. We had to pass one another to get past the bar. Pause — at this very moment I had two choices — stand there and keep my mouth shut or speak and be the bigger person.

I spoke and said hello. I really believe the girl was waiting for me to speak so that she could offer a negative reaction. Or perhaps she was just that miserable of a person that she purposely planted herself at the bar to stir up some trouble at my expense.

She did not disappoint. She delivered the negativity that I expected. I looked up and said "Hi" and here is what happened next: She looked down her nose at me and grunted a "don't speak to me" and walked away.

Was I upset about her response? Well, for about 10 seconds, I was, and I will tell you why: The woman is over 40 years old and I would have expected a better response from her as an elder (insert laugh here). No but seriously. Here is a woman who was constantly promoting 'girl power' but did not practice what she preached. On top of that I had no idea how I had wronged this girl.

I wasn't upset at what she did but upset that she was not woman enough to pull me aside and let me know that she had a problem with me and why she had that problem. Even more disappointing was the fact that she chose a mutual friend's birthday party to try and make a scene.

This is one of the problems with us women today —
we have a cut-throat mentality and a crabs-in-a-barrel
syndrome going on. We as women do hateful things to
one another and it has got to stop.

You all know the story, you have heard the story a
million times and a million different ways:

- Girl 1 and Girl 2 find out they are dating the same
  man. Instead of Girl 1 going to confront the man,
  she wages an all-out war on Girl 2 for dating the
  same man. Meanwhile Girl 2 had no idea that the
  man was even taken. Why is Girl 1 mad at Girl 2?
  Girl 2 had no idea that this man was playing the
  field. Girl 1's real beef should be with the low life
  man they were both dating; not with Girl 2.

- Girl 1 and Girl 2 both work at the same job. For
  whatever reason Girl 1 does not like Girl 2.
  Perhaps it is because Girl 2 is in a higher position
  at work, or maybe Girl 2 is respected more at
  work and Girl 1 is lazy, always late to work and
  never completes an assignment on time. Instead
  of changing her work ethic, Girl 1 finds that it is
  easier just to make it difficult at work for Girl 2.

I think you get the point!

Don't get me wrong, you will not LOVE everyone you come in contact with. Not everyone will even LIKE you. There will not be a "rah, rah, sis boom bah" vibe for everyone you meet but that does not mean you cannot respect that person as an individual. All of the **energy** that my 'hater' took to roll her eyes, make that comment and walk away — where did it get her? I am still standing, you did not affect my happiness, health, job or children so why act like that? To vindicate yourself? Perhaps low self-esteem?

I am not sure why people react the way that they do and it is not my job to figure it out. For every action there is a reaction but I choose not to react. Suppose I did react and started an argument with her and we started fighting or had a screaming match in front of everyone at the party? I am getting a vision here of us rolling on the floor, weaves pulled out, bra straps ripped – you get the idea. What would that have gotten us both? A free ride in the back of a police car, fines, a court date or unnecessary drama?

Instead I cut the drama off at the pass and did not respond and for that I am the bigger person. Besides, I have too much going on to be scuffing my knees up wrestling on the floor with that monster of a woman.

Plus, I'm super cute so I don't need my face scratched up. (Had to smile at that).

Blessed

To whom much is given, much is required. I have led a blessed life for the most part and I felt it was my duty to show others how I did it. I want other mothers to feel like they can do it also. Just because you have a child at a young age does not mean your dreams have to stop. Nor does it mean that you cannot be successful in life. You may just have to take a different path than most; a carefully crafted path that I can help you plan. If you fail to plan then you plan to fail; plain and simple. I am sure I'm t5not telling you anything that you have not heard in the past.

It is at the ripe age of 39 as I write this book that I find it is my calling to take a risk and put myself out there and help others to be encouraged and successful in life. So many people are afraid to take risks for various reasons: Perhaps they do not have the resources or are simply afraid of failure. With the right attitude you can do anything you envision in life. "Faith without works is dead." In other words, you can have all the faith, faith that is deeper than the Grand Canyon, but if you do not exhibit the actions to back up that faith, you are not going to get very far.

Let's face it, no one walks around and says, "I can't make it. I'm going to be a failure in life!" Everyone wants to make it but lack the wherewithal to do something about it. So, they give up.

Let me just warn you that this will be no means be an easy task. There will be people that may discourage you and tell you not to make a plan to advance in life. There will be days when you wake out of bed and feel like giving up. There will be people that mock you because they do not understand your bigger plan. It is human nature for people to not accept that which they cannot understand. Just keep going on your journey and don't stop!

If you have a bad day, there is always tomorrow to restart your journey. If you have a bad week, there is always next week to restart your journey. Many times just a hug from my children or even a gaze in their innocent faces would be enough reinforcement for me to know that I could not give up; for their sake.

Not everyone has people in their corner rooting for them every step of the way. Nor do they have people there to tell them me not to give up. But there also has to be that inner drive that one possesses that makes him or her not want to give up, a driving thirst to achieve a goal. A thirst to take their plan to the next level.

My sincere hope is that the words in this book will inspire you to want better for your life, to be thought-provoking and hopefully to serve as a springboard to jumpstart your life, whether you are a divorced mother or you are a single mother looking for the right direction, or you're just looking for some consoling words as you forge ahead, this book is for you.

Too often with single motherhood the onus is placed on one person to raise a child or children and at the same time to maintain a career and her sanity. I am here to tell you that it can be done. It will not be easy all of the time but it is achievable and will be well worth it in the end.

Lastly, I always believed in paying it forward. Once you are successful in life you should reach down and pull others up and help them be successful as well. If in your lifetime you can reach one person and make a change in their life for the better then you have achieved a great feat.

The Take-Aways:

- Remain positive

- Always take the high road

- Live a life of purpose!

- Don't sweat the small stuff; after all....it's just small stuff

"Our greatest weakness lies in giving up. The most certain way to succeed is to always try just one more time". – *Thomas A. Edison*

Picture courtesy wanttobeseen.net

CHAPTER 2
SETTING MEASURABLE GOALS

God won't give you more than you can handle. I do not proclaim to know the Bible back and forth, nor am I a 'holy roller,' but I will say that I am a Christian woman and try to the best of my ability to lead a respectful life. Have there been times where I did things that I am not proud of? Of course; who hasn't? I would be lying to you if I told you that I have always walked the straight and narrow.

I will say that when you make mistakes you learn from them. If you commit the same mistake again, it's no longer a mistake – just a foolish move on your part. One time is enough for me to learn a lesson and life will bring you plenty of lessons. In life you must have a plan and you must put that plan to use. As a matter of fact you must have a backup plan and it would not hurt to have a backup plan to the backup plan.

Set measurable goals as you work through each step in your plan. In this section I will tell you how to put a plan in place and make it work. Yes, you may stumble along the way and yes even fall down a time or two. Each time you fall down, you have not failed; unless you fail to get back up and try again.

I remember when I was attending community college and working part time at the same time. I knew that I was half way to receiving my associate degree in business and I was not going to let anything stop me. Each semester when the class schedule would come out I would sit at the table with a pen, the schedule, and a blank sheet of paper. I would creatively figure out how I would take 3 or more credits and work part time.

I even went to my boss and told her my plan. She knew I was a single parent and she was more than accommodating to me as I worked my way through community college and balanced being a mother at the same time.

Many times in my life I managed to be in the right place at the right time. I do not know if I was just blessed or if I was lucky. I was very much afraid to approach my boss and ask for permission to attend school around my work schedule but I had decided that the worst that could happen was rejection. I mean it was not like my boss was going to throw me up against the wall and start thrashing me for asking a simple question. There were two options; she could say yes or she could say no. As it turned out she said yes!

Then there was another obstacle, I was given permission to attend college during my work day but I did not have a definite way to get there! At the time I did not have a car and currently rode the bus to work. If I was going to make this work I had better get real creative. I remember one weekend I thought long and hard about how I was going to make this work. I went through every scenario in my mind on how I was going to make this work. I am a visual person, so it is helpful to me to see things written down.

With bus schedule in hand I painstakingly scheduled each work and school day. I managed to successfully plan out my work and school schedule for each day of the week. I also called Human Services in our town to find out if there were any resources for working mothers. It turned out that there was a taxi service available for working moms that I could use free of charge. Between the buses, the taxi service, the affirmation from my boss and my can-do attitude I was set! So there you have it. I did not give up, I sat and racked my brain to put a plan together and figure out how I was going to manage this very important facet of my life. This was just one of my many plans that I would put together. Now it's your turn.

So let's put a plan together for your life; exciting stuff! Come on, get excited! Don't be intimidated by thinking a plan has to be a two hundred page double spaced document. A plan can be one paragraph.

So now I'm getting a visual of you sitting at a table with a pen and a piece of paper with your hand in the air like "now what?" Please do not worry or overwhelm yourself with trying to come up with a plan to fix your life and get you on your way. If it were that easy you would have done it already. A plan is nothing more than a set of goals with measurable steps in between to help you progress to your next goal. For instance let me provide you with an example.

Let's just say one of the big goals in your life is to buy a house. In a perfect world, the measurable steps one may take in order to buy a house are as follows:

1. Order a credit score to determine what your actual credit score is and view items which may hurt my chances of securing a mortgage and a decent interest rate.

2. Research potential areas in which you may want to purchase a home. This includes researching crime rates and school systems if you have children.

3. Visit banks and have a casual talk with a mortgage office to determine qualifications for obtaining a mortgage. It will not cost you a dime to have a conversation with a bank employee and they should be happy to assist a potential customer. If you find that this is not the case then you are in the wrong bank; move right along to the next bank.

4. Research housing grants to determine eligibility.

5. Research affordable housing organizations to determine if you are eligible for assistance in buying a home.

6. Save every bit of money for a down payment and other housing costs associated with buying a home. This may include possibly obtaining a second job in order to work toward a sizeable down payment.

7. Having a realistic talk with yourself to determine if you financially and emotionally are ready to take on the responsibility of homeownership.

Let me issue a disclaimer here and tell you that I am not a mortgage expert and what I have outlined is merely an example of smaller measurable steps to take toward the bigger goal of purchasing a home.

So the first step you would take here would be to take a piece of paper and jot down some goals that you would like to achieve over the next few years. Some of my goals in the past have been as follows:

➢ Purchasing a home
➢ Obtaining an MBA
➢ Obtaining a job that would provide me with a six figure income.

At the risk of bragging, I am happy to report that I have accomplished all three of these goals! It had taken me at least ten plus years to complete all three but I did not give up until I did! And you can do the same! This book would be eight hundred pages long if I gave you the long version of how I did it. I will say that I got sick and tired of being sick and tired. I fell down and off track many times but I would always start over and try it again. I will give you the short version instead to get you started.

Sit down and get a piece of a paper and determine what you would like to accomplish in your life for this week, this month, year or even five years from now. Write these goals down but leave some space underneath to make notes and track your progress.

In the space underneath the goals, write down tasks or steps that you need to perform in order to complete the goal. It may even be helpful to write down the time frame in which you would like to achieve the goal.

Anything in life has certain steps to get to the end result. Nothing just happens! There are always steps leading up to an end result.

Some people are visual creatures and I understand that. If you feel better having a visual representation of your goals visit your local dollar store and buy a piece of poster board. Make a collage of the things that you envision yourself doing or having in the years to come. This is called a vision board and has become very popular in the past few years.

Whether you create a vision board or write your goals on a piece of paper, paste your goals on a wall that you walk past each day like your refrigerator or your car dashboard. Let it serve as a constant reminder of what you are trying to achieve on a daily basis. Good luck and have fun with this project! The page that follows will provide you some examples of goal setting.

MY GOAL(S)

1. _____

   What I need to accomplish this (measurable tasks)

   ➤ _____

      ○ _____ *(sometimes tasks*
         need to be broken down)

   ➤ _____

   Comments

   _____

MY GOAL

1. To chew gum and walk at the same time

   ➤ What I need to accomplish this (measurable tasks):
     - Ensure my mouth is clear of other food
     - Obtain a long lasting pack of gum
       - Place a piece of gum inside my mouth
       - Start chewing

   ➤ Wear comfortable walking shoes
     - Ensure the shoes are tied and are easy to walk in
     - Have lots of patience

   ➤ If at first I do not succeed—Try try again!

   ➤ Take my first step

   Comments: It was easier than I thought!

I know what you are thinking. Why did she provide an example of chewing gum and walking at the same time? I will tell you. I was making light of the situation but at the same time showing you how simple creating a plan can be. We all know how to chew gum and walk at the same time therefore coming up with a plan is a task that anyone can undertake.

Making a plan is like following a recipe to make a cake. You find out what you need to do and then step by step you make the cake! Now that I have beat that topic like a dead horse let us move on.

The Take-Aways:

o Every first BIG step begins with baby steps.

o Fall down 3 times, get up a 4th time and keep going.

o Have a Plan A, B, C and X!

o Fail to plan; then you plan to fail!

"Money is a tool. Used properly it makes something beautiful- used wrong, it makes a mess!"
— *Bradley Vinson*

CHAPTER 3
MONEY MANAGEMENT 101

I know firsthand that using money improperly can make a mess of things and boy oh boy have I made a mess of my finances in the past. For many people, managing finances and ensuring your financial wellbeing is in good order is like second nature. Sadly for myself this was not the case. Like many things in life, if you are not taught or never experience certain things in life you either find out by trial and error or you never find out. Let's just say that credit and finance was something I learned by trial and error.

Many times I lived very materialistically and believed that having nice clothes, making non-essential purchases and partying every weekend was more important than actually saving for the future and investing.

Many times I moved into apartments and I knew full well that there was no way I could afford to pay the rent. I would move in and figured everything would fall in place at a later time. I was not honest with myself and I knew darn well that my expenses outweighed my income. This is not the way to live life and over time becomes a very stressful situation. Having to take time off of work in order to attend court hearings or renting a truck in order to move furniture because of eviction is no fun. Let's just say I was not making the wisest decisions at that point in my life in regard to many things; money was one of them.

For many years in my life I had been going in circles and having terrible financial woes and neglecting my financial situation. Through all my trials and tribulations I was the best mother to my kids that I ever could have been. I did whatever it took to put food in my children's mouth and make sure they never did without. I say all that to say, I would never want anyone to follow the long and twisted path I took to where I am today. Sometimes if people know how to do something the right way the first time they don't have to go around in a circle and waste time. There is a saying "If you know better; you do better." This is so true. I wasted many years of my life doing the wrong things with my money. I learned some hard lessons, oh how I learned! I got sick and tired of being sick and tired of broke!

I woke up one day and said, "Am I going to sit here and cry a river about this debt or am I going to get up off my butt and do something about it?" I was determined to look into fixing my credit and get on the road to financial recovery. I searched and was successful in teaming up with a credit counseling agency. Over the course of two years they helped me pay my debtors. I also checked out books from the library and learned how to set up a budget and gathered ideas for money management from an magazine I could get my hands on. I also talked to friends and family members that I knew were great savers! This goes back to the point I made in the previous chapter--- talk to people that have done it and been successful at it!

Saving Money

You know, I have never been very good at saving money, I will be honest. But I got better at it. By no means will I sit here and lecture you and tell you that you should have thousands of dollars in the bank because I myself have to work hard at saving money on a daily basis; even to this day. Someg things are just to be taken one day at a time and that is fine. Don't overwhelm yourself with thinking that being good at saving money is something that occurs overnight. Are you tired of living paycheck to paycheck? If not, at some point you will be.

I know, I know, you have heard it millions of times:

"You need three months' worth of expenses saved up in the event of an emergency"…yada yada yada! The fact is that you need to save money in the event that the rainy day comes! Don't get caught out there. If you fail to plan then you plan to fail, point blank. There are some very easy ways to save money that I learned over the years and I can give you some pointers.

By no means am I a Suze Orman or a financial guru but hopefully I can give you some pointers to get you started. I can tell you some things that have worked for me.

One way I have learned to save money is by putting aside a set amount of money each pay period that goes into a separate account. I have set up a separate savings account and I have my company deposit the money directly from my paycheck into the separate account so that I never see it. Out of sight, out of mind. There have been times that I forget about that account with that extra money coming out. Before you know it, it will build and build and you will have a nice rainy-day fund.

If you do not have the option of a direct deposit from your job, you can always deposit the money yourself into a separate bank account. The trick is that this money should not be touched under any circumstances. Holding out on spending money will be difficult but I promise you it will pay off in the end.

One of the best things that you can do with your money is to contribute to any retirement or 401K plan that your job offers. Many jobs also match employees' contributions up to a certain percentage. There are also other vehicles in which to save, like a Roth IRA, which enables your money to earn interest while you contribute. Here are some other tips that I am sure you have all heard before. A little reminder can't hurt:

- Eat out less. Eating at home is healthier and may save you in hospital bills in the long run.

- Watch financial programs like Suze Orman and David Ramsey. I love Suze and she always uses practical life situations. This always encourages me to handle my money more responsibly. Dave Ramsey has that in-your-face type of personality and sometimes that is exactly what is needed.

- There are lots of websites like Calendarforkids.com that post free events in your area for the kiddies. Or watch the social networks and local newspapers for free and family-friendly activities.

- Go the park with the kids, or the library to check out books for free. I always enjoyed visiting the library with my kids. The library offers so many activities like movies and book readings.

- Keep up with car maintenance. If you take care of your car it will take care of you. Then you don't need to worry about large mechanic bills down the line.

Another very smart way to track the money you are spending on a monthly basis is by keeping a budget. A budget is very easy to set up and is just a matter of tracking the amount of money going out of your household (expenses) in comparison to the money coming into your household (income).

For your convenience I have included an example of a budget on the page that follows that I use to track my monthly expenses. The key here is to be honest with yourself about what you are spending. Keep track of everything! No expense is too small to keep track of.

This budget is merely an example and your budget will be different. The important part here is that you are tracking where your money is going. Good luck!

Item	Cost
Daycare	300
Gas/Tolls	60
Car Payment	210
Utility Bills	120
Mortgage	1100
Cellular	60
Cable Bundle	60
Sewage Bill	30
Groceries	300
Dining Out	30
Hair cuts/ Nails	150
Misc	50
Life Insurance Policy	20
Pet Expenses	30
Savings	200
Clothes	20
Summer Vacation	73
Expenses	**2893**
Income	**3500**
Money left after expenses	**607**

Reading is fundamental

Yes, knowledge is power, make it your purpose to read at least one financial book or magazine per year. The problem with many people of my generation is that we don't read. We would rather look at television or the internet to get all of our information than to pick up a book and actually learn something. I love to read and I do so often. I am just the type of person that has a thirst for knowledge and I love learning. Not only can you learn from reading but it can only add to your vocabulary and strengthen your brain muscles.   In this age of technology we humans are using our brains less and less. I don't know about you but I like to think for myself from time to time rather than have a computer or machine do it for me.

Remember there are many ways to read in this day and age. This includes the Kindle, Nook or even downloading an application to your smart phone which allows you to read from the comfort of your phone. Many times I even listen to books on my long drive to work via Audible.com. If you are unfamiliar, Audible is an application which you can download to your smart phone that will actually read the book to you while you listen along. Not only can I listen to books while I am driving but I can also listen while cleaning, having some alone time in the bathroom away from children, and when cooking.

I know what you are saying – "I don't have the time to read a book." Well make the time. People will make time for the things that they really want to do. Bring a book along while the kids are playing sports and you are sitting in the bleachers. Or during your "me" time, after the kiddies are all tucked in and sound asleep, pull out that money management article from Essence magazine that you have been putting off reading since last week

Yes, buying books and magazines can become very costly. Thank goodness there is still such a place which nearly every town has called The Public Library that still offers free books and magazines for our reading pleasure!

Keeping up with the Joneses

I used to be very materialistic. I wanted to keep up with any and everything that my friends and others that i saw were doing. I wanted to make sure I wore the best designer tags and any pocketbook on my arm had better be designer. Never mind the fact that my car was on the verge of being repossessed. Or that my rent was 2 months behind. I was not concerned with those things. I needed to look good and in my mind that was all that mattered. I would take my entire income tax and go shopping for all of the latest clothes and sneakers for me and my kids. Girl, that rent would have to wait.

That was back in the late nineties when there was no Facebook or Instagram to showcase on. I can't even imagine what I would have been posting had Facebook been in existence back then.

Fast forward to the year 2014. Blooow!! This is the millennium of everything in your face! Everything is just a click away from being yours! As I scroll through my Facebook and Instagram pages I see friends taking lavish trips to the Caribbean, the latest Prada pocketbook that this friend just purchased, new townhouse purchased by this friend, this friend jut copped a brand new C- Class Mercedes Benz; you get the point. In a previous life I would have been plotting on how I was going to do the same as soon as I got my hot little hands on the money. But now I know better. I also know that a large percentage of the folks posting this information on social media cannot afford these items and have no savings in the bank to protect themselves and their family in the event of a rainy day.

Please don't be fooled by what people are claiming on social media. A lot of claims may very well be true but many of the claims may have been purchased as a result of neglecting other financial obligations. This type of behavior will eventually catch up to the person. On Facebook, Twitter or Instagram you can portray yourself to be and have anything you want people to believe! So be cautious, believe none of what you hear and only half of what you read or see on social media.

Reality TV

The reality of reality television is that most of what you are seeing on reality television is far from reality. How many times have we watched one of these television shows only to learn a few years later that one of the reality stars was broke and filing for bankruptcy? Exactly.

I see women immulate these characters and begin to dress and act like the person on the reality show; even looking up to the person as a role model. Stop. This is television and is for entertainment purposes. These people are being paid to live this falsehood. Many of these lavish homes and cars are rented for purposes of the show and are not actually owned by the reality stars.

Furthermore, stop trying to live someone else's reality and live your own reality. Stand in your own truth and financial circumstances. It is nice to dream about living a certain lifestyle and with time, patience and good money management a nice lifestyle can certainly be achieved; possibly even as nice as those seen on these reality television shows.

Nothing worth having comes easy so yes you will need to work at wealth. In the meantime it's nice to watch reality television and laugh at the story lines. I love reality television and I have my favorites that I tune into on any given day but I know that their reality is different from mine.

+

The Take-Aways:

o The harder you work now at becoming financially fit, the better off you will be in years to come

o Save ! Save ! Save!

o Be honest with yourself about money!

o Stop trying to keep up with the Joneses. The Joneses can't even keep up with themselves.

CHAPTER 4
PLAN A, B, C AND X!

It takes a village

It is so important to have a support system while you going this alone. Unfortunately, in my case I did not always have family readily available to assist in cases of emergencies with my children. I have friends whose parents are retired or make themselves available to help out with their grandchildren at all times. I always envied that and never had that luxury.

In some cases, maybe you do have parents or other relatives, but, guess what? They don't offer to even lend a hand. Or perhaps cannot lend a hand because they themselves have work commitments. Don't be upset at this. After all, you choose to have these children so they are your responsibility.

I used to get so upset when I would call others for help to no avail. Then I realized if someone wants to help you or provide a helping hand, guess what? They will. I then came up with several emergency plans as a support system for my children.

I stopped being afraid to ask people for a helping hand. If you ask a person for help the worst they can say is no. I mean it's not like they will reach out and slap you for asking. Well, I hope not. People usually try to help out when they are able especially if they know you are trying to improve your life.

Don't get me wrong, there were plenty of family and friends that helped out when they could but there was no one steady on my support team for several years. I had to realize that everyone had other responsibilities and could not help me at that time. There was also a time when I paid people whom I had entrusted to watch my children while I either worked or attended school.

I was blessed to have had people referred to me to watch my children whom I learned to entrust and ended up being excellent babysitters to my children. If you decide to take this route you will need to be very cautious and mindful of who you let into your home. I interviewed potential babysitters like it was a criminal interrogation. I did not play with my children's safety. I did thorough background and reference checks.

If you do not have options, you have to make options. Maybe you may have a neighbor that can be of help or perhaps you can pay a high school student to assist when necessary. Perhaps you can team up with other single mothers in your position and use the barter system or take turns helping out with one another's kids.

Use your resources. Check your local county office to find out what childcare resources may be available to you. If you do not have the luxury of your parents helping out with your children then you have to not only have a Plan A, but a Plan B, a Plan C and a Plan X as well.

Join the PTA or get to know the neighborhood mothers. You never know, there may be a mom, single or married, who is looking for that extra help and you two could serve as a resource to one another. You have to be creative. If you are a member of your church, talk to your Pastor and ask him if you can set up a single mothers' ministry; single mothers mentoring one another under the tutelage of a minister — what could be better?

Check with your local Human Services Department and sign up for any child care programs there. Also ask for a list of referrals of local babysitters which are certified by the state to care for children. Many times there are often child care grants or stipends that single moms can take advantage of as well.

There may be a time where these resources are not available to you, meaning you may need to pay a person to help with the care of your children like I did. If this is the case then perhaps there is a high school student or neighborhood teen looking to make extra money. Employ him or her.

In any case, please be careful about the people that you are entrusting with the care of your child. Hardly anything in life is ever predictable but you need to go with your instincts as with anything. If something is giving you a bad feeling or taste in your mouth then you are probably right; something is wrong!

Also, listen to the cues that your children are giving you with anything. Children will usually tell or exhibit behavior to let you know when something is wrong. So whatever route you choose, be careful!

Scheduling life

My life is a schedule, literally. Don't feel bad for me. It might sound sad but actually it is the best thing that I could ever do for myself. I literally schedule my entire day; to make sure I don't run out of day! Sounds crazy I know but this is the only way I know of how to function and not forget important tasks. In my mind if I don't write it down it never happened! Listen I am a woman of a certain age and they say the first thing to go is the memory. And in my case this is true! I tend to forget many things and so I need to either write things down and schedule appointments in my smart phone or write it down manually on a calendar. I also have the habit of turning up late to appointments so if I schedule appointments out I have the tendency to actually show up on time. It is a win -win situation for all involved; I am on time and I haven't forgotten.

The Take-Aways:

- ○ Have a plan, a backup plan, and a backup plan to the backup plan!

- ○ Build a support network

- ○ Write it down, write it down, write it down

CHAPTER 5
UNLOCKING THE KEYS TO SUCCESS

Career Training and Education

Hey, let's face it: College is not for everyone, but in this day in age you need to think about a long-term career to support you and your family. Whether it be entrepreneurship, college or a trade school. Or perhaps you may want to look to get hired at a utility company, become a policewoman, or just find a job with a solid future that will offer a 401K plan and/or a pension. Long gone are the days in which our parents lived, when we signed on with one company and worked there our entire lives.

In the workplace you need a specialized skill that will set you apart from the pack. I see so many women that don't take getting some kind of education seriously and end up in dead-end jobs.

There are always trade schools at which you may learn a skill to make a living or vocational schools where you can obtain a vocational license. Love what you do every time you get out of that bed and head to work. It will make it all the more worthwhile.

If you decide down the line that you would like to attend college; then attend college. Stop making excuses – "I don't have time, I can't afford it or I'm too old". There are many options for attending college that were not available when I was attending college. There are countless ways to earn a college degree like online colleges, colleges that offer weekend programs or the good old fashioned option of walking into a classroom in an actual building. There are also many educational grants available in particular to working moms looking to further their education. You would be surprised at the demographics of student in a college classroom. I attended college with people of all ages and we all had one thing in common; we were there to learn.

Suppose you decide that school is not for you at this time. That is fine as well. I have seen many mothers attend college or learn a trade after their children have left home or started high school. No one can tell you when the right time is to further your education but you. I must also warn you that many companies are beginning to require its employees to have a Bachelor's degree at the least to even work in the mailroom.

You are probably wondering how you will pay for an education or further job training. If you are employed, check with your workplace; perhaps they will pay for your school tuition in full or offer reimbursement for a portion of your education.

Also, check with the local unemployment office if you are jobless. Many times the state will pay for job training. In addition, check with your local human resources agency to find out if there are grants or programs that will aid you in furthering your knowledge.

If you choose not to college or a trade school, work on getting a job and the experience to make you valuable to the company. A company will think twice about getting rid of you if they feel like you are an asset to the company or possess a certain skill that is invaluable to them.

No one should ever make you feel like less of a woman because you do not possess a college education. Many of the world's most successful people like Shirley Bassey, Mary Kay Ash, Lady Gaga, Coco Chanel, and Debbi Fields never possessed a college degree but that did not stop them from moving on to live a life of greatness.

There are a few relatives in my family that never finished high school but went on to own their own businesses and were successful at it.

My father is a living example of the fact that, somewhere out there, there is work for everyone. My Dad did not go to college or trade school and has worked for himself for the majority of his life. He has honed a skill and created a business which that fed his family and paid his bills for the majority of my life. So don't say that there are no jobs—create a job or a hustle. Get creative! What is your talent? What do you enjoy doing? What is there a need for in your community? As the saying goes, as long as you love what you do, you will always have a job. I wholeheartedly believe that.

Some of you will say, "There are just no jobs out here. I'm educated and I cannot find a job to save my life." Or "I've been out here looking every day and I am having no luck." I get it, there were be a percentage of you that will not have any luck whatsoever at finding gainful employment. I was never the one to give up so easily at anything so I will not let you give up either.

There are many resources available to you in your community. Reach out to your local Human Services Department and Unemployment Office for employment referrals. Scan the newspapers, magazines and Craig's List for potential leads. Also helpful are the online job database like Monster and CareerBuilder. Put it out there on LinkedIn, Facebook and Twitter or even Instagram . The old fashioned word of mouth is also a potential job finder. My previous job was gotten due to a referral from a past coworker.

Last of all, if you have to make the choice between your family starving and you beating your feet to the pavement to find a job--- most of you, I hope, will beat the pavement. If all else fails, McDonald's is always hiring.

Workplace Mommas

Thank goodness many companies these days are providing a life/work balance for its employees. I am happy to say that I am currently employed at one of these companies. My company understands that all though the company needs to turn a profit at the end of the day, its employees have lives outside of work. There are certain incentives which make my current employer attractive like vacation and sick days, the option to work from home when needed, an open door policy for management,

Employee Appreciation Events, bonus plans, a retirement plan which is company matched, Bring Your Child To Work Day; to name a few. They get it! They are definitely a new millennium company and understand that in order to ensure employee productivity is at a maximum they must keep their employees happy. My company is definitely the exception to the rule and I am blessed to be employed with this company.

In a perfect world every employer would take into consideration its employees work and life balance but we do not live in a perfect world so one must make the best of their work situation. If you cannot change something then change the way you think about it. If your employer is not offering you the flexibility of a work life balance then you will need to make the best of your situation.

Another option is perhaps even making suggestions to your human resource company or manager on how to make the company a more comfortable place to work. If you choose this option be prepared to submit a well written plan so that they take your suggestions serious. Solicit feedback from your coworkers so that you have support.

If you feel as though you are not being heard or are undervalued then perhaps it may be time for you to look for another job opportunity. Do not take this decision lightly. This will take a lot of thought and preparation on your part. I would never advise anyone to just up and quit a job without careful thought and consideration.

Girl, Get Your Body and Mind Right!

I believe spiritual healing and exercise may go hand in hand. It is a complete package. Girl, get your body right! Exercise, exercise, exercise! You have lot on your shoulders as a single parent, we want to make sure you are in the best physical shape possible. Your body is a temple; worship it and your body will thank you for it as well! Studies have shown that exercise boosts energy levels and drastically reduces the likelihood for certain diseases like diabetes and hypertension.

As I write this book I must say that I always, always struggled with my weight. My weight was like a yo-yo — up and down, up and down. I had tried all of the diets — Weight Watchers, South Beach, you name it, I had tried it or at least a variation of it.

I became frustrated as I spent hundreds of dollars trying different diets and copying diets that others were having success with. I even contemplated having bypass surgery but found out that I was not a candidate for it.

Yes, that was lazy of me but I soon realized that there was no easy way out of this weight issue. If I wanted to have a successful weight-loss journey then I would need to put the work in plain and simple.

The fact is that everyone has a different weight loss journey. No one journey is the identical. You must experiment and do what works for you. The thing that seemed to work best for me was calorie counting and watching my portion sizes in addition to exercise.

Finally I decided to buckle down and try to tackle this thing on my own; after all, I was on the heels of 40 and I wanted to look fab before my 40th birthday! Also, I wanted to get in shape because I'd heard that as you get older it is harder to lose weight. After the birth of my second child I had also come down with high blood pressure or what is medically called hypertension. My doctor promised that if had lost a considerable amount of weight there was a possibility for me to ditch my hypertension medicine.

I cut certain foods out of my diet, like breads, carbohydrates, pasta and soda. I did not want to deprive myself so I was good during the week with this regimen and then ate whatever I wanted to on the weekends. This way I had something to look forward to and it didn't seem too terrible. I also spent at least thirty minutes on the treadmill walking at least four times per week.

At the time of this book I had already lost ten pounds and was proud of what I had accomplished. I was not able to ditch my hypertension medication just yet but I am still working toward that goal. I cannot say enough, everyone's weight-loss journey is different and everyone's body is different. What works for one will not work for all. You have to figure out what works for you. I would also suggest contacting your physician to ensure that they have no objections to any type of weight-loss regimen that you undertake.

I continue to struggle with staying at a healthy weight. I never wanted to return to the same weight I was in high school (I was a stick). However, I do wish to be healthy and that does not mean being a stick figure. Don't believe the hype and television shows that say you have to be 'skinty'(skinny) in order to be healthy. In addition, many of those television celebrities have had surgeries, personal trainers, or sometimes even private chefs to help them maintain their looks.

Before you can get your life completely together you must get your health together. That includes eating right and making sure you are healthy. I have found that healthy eating has become a lifestyle for me. It has not been easy but I will not give up. Some people are just so blessed that they can eat just about anything and never gain a pound. Unfortunately, I am not one of those folks. A moment on the lips equals a lifetime on the hips is what they say. So don't be discouraged. Do what is best for you!

It is imperative that you also get at least eight hours of sleep in order to function the next day. Long gone are the days of my early twenties when I would be out at the club until 2am, come home and get 4 hour worth of sleep and still be able to get up and go to work with no problem.

Visiting your doctor at least once per year and the dentist every six months is also important. If you do not have health insurance many hospitals have clinics that will see you for free. Do not take your health for granted. Yearly doctor check-ups will be able to detect any diseases and head off any medical issues in the early stages. You have a lot on your plate as a single mother so you must make time to ensure your health is in order.

There are plenty of plus-sized women that eat healthily and have a little more meat on their bones but are considered by their doctors to be completely healthy! Again, everyone's body is different and you must do what is best for you and not concern yourself with what everyone else is doing. If you feel good in the skin you are in and are happy with your size, and you are healthy well that is cool too!

Spirituality

In my opinion, spirituality is something that everyone should have. I don't care if you are Muslim, Christian or a Scientologist; everyone needs to be at one with the higher levels of the universe. Having a connection with a higher being just makes you a better person, it gives you humility and understanding of all things. I know for myself that going to church to hear "the word" makes me better equipped to handle anything that comes my way.

I am a firm believer in God and I do attend church on occasion. That does not mean one has to be in church Monday through Sunday in order to be considered a Christian. I hear some pearls being clutched right now but the truth is that you cannot judge my walk with God based on the way I choose to worship. Many people choose other ways to worship over walking into a church every Sunday morning and that is fine; that is between them and The Lord. Surely you believe there is a high power controlling the universe even if you don't believe in God, right?

Whatever your preference is when it comes to religion remember to keep an open mind. Be open to learning about other's religion. I know some people that have even converted to other religions. Most importantly, do not judge someone because they worship differently than you.

Get to know yourself if you do not know yourself already. I mean that in all aspects! Sometimes we get lost, whether it is in work, relationships, outside family situations. The list goes on. It's time for you to get back to you, starting today. When I was laid off from work in 2011 I had nothing but time on my hands. I got to know ME.

I spent lots of time walking on the beach, reading books, watching the OWN Network, meditating and just spending time with myself. And it really worked! I emerged a different person after I took time out for myself and took the time to breathe in the air and really evaluate what was going on in my life. I am glad I used that time I was laid off to get back to me in a positive way.

I hear some woman say that they would never go out to dinner by themselves or never attend a movie alone. That is the most ridiculous thing I have ever heard. That tells me that you have low self-esteem. That you are afraid to go any place for fear that others would judge you for being alone. Why would you not go out into the world because you need a whole entourage in order to eat dinner or take a walk on the beach? How can you take time out for yourself if you always have someone accompanying you everywhere you go? It just takes away from the whole purpose of getting to know 'you'.

The times I spent 'dolo' or alone were some of the best soul searching times for me. Those were the times when the light bulb clicked on in that attic of a brain of mind. I will really lost for a lot of years with no sense of direction. Between the years of 2007 through 2012 were probably some of my most miserable working years that I can recall.

I was in a job with a manager that was absolutely spiteful for new reason. The working conditions were horrible. Everyone hated it there, but we stayed because we were getting paid well. Don't get me wrong, every job will not be peaches and cream and have the best managers. I get that. But this job was full of managers that were micro-managing and not interested in the least bit in the betterment of their employees.

My manager would often discourage any step I would take in elevating my position, yet she would always tell me that I could come and talk to her about anything. She had an open door policy she said. Obviously that was not the case and a contradiction.

I can recall that at that time I was enrolled in an online school working toward my MBA. Many times my manager would take months to sign off on a request for college reimbursement and even one time refused to sign off. Needless to say that time I went over her head to Human Resources and she had no choice but to sign off.

I remember she even discouraged me for applying within the company for other positions. I bided my time and very patiently. In my mind I needed money to pay my mortgage and to take care of my children. I knew that to gain a better job in my industry that I needed an MBA. So I toughed it out got my degree and patiently waited for my exit.

Each Sunday night my stomach would start to churn in anticipation of the work week ahead. I would pull up the job site in the morning and automatically have an instant attitude. To get over this feeling I did little things to get me through the day like taking a 15 minute break in afternoon and then again in the evening. A nice stroll may relax the tension and give you a clear mind. At lunch I would go sit in my car and listen to music. It is amazing how a song off of the Mary J. Blige album My Life can get you through the day. I did whatever it was to be able to deal with my boss and the job. I made the best of a miserable situation.

One day another manager came up to me. I won't mention her name but she informed me that she had resigned from the company and was moving on to greener pastures. I was very elated for her, gave her a hug and wished her the best. This manger knew that I had gotten my MBA by that time and that I was also searching for a new job.

This manager told me to be patient and hold off, that the company was undergoing a reorganization. She said that perhaps if I were to be laid off I could take some time off and move on to a better job and enjoy a nice severance while I waited on that dream job. The manager also told me that I was worth more than the treatment that I was getting under my current manager. She was right. Needless to say that was happened next was worth the wait! My life would be forever changed.

Getting laid off from work was probably one of the best things to happen to me because it gave me the time to find myself again.

The Take-Aways:

○ Carve out a career for yourself

○ If you cannot change a situation, change the way you think about that situation.

○ Your body is a temple, worship it.

○ When one door closes five more doors open up.

"Insanity: doing the same thing over and over again and expecting different results". –
Albert Einstein

CHAPTER 6
BABY MOMMA NO DRAMA

Don't be bitter, be better. This book is by no means intended for male-bashing. I truly believe that a child needs both parents in his or her life if that is at all possible.

When I had my children I never intended for it to be a one woman show. But, life happens. When I parted ways with my first child's father, I was extremely bitter. I was very upset when our relationship ended for the mere fact that he was my first true love and I wanted to raise our child in a two parent household like the household in which I had been raised.

There were so many feelings and emotions coupled with the fact that I was a new mother and possibly going through postpartum depression. I was actually engaged to be married to my child's father but a ring and a brand new baby did not stop him from ending our relationship. I was stunned, I wanted answers and kept reliving our relationship in my head trying to figure if there was something I could have done better. I was trying to figure out how I could reverse the break-up.

Each time I would see him I would get a false hope thinking that by giving him my body I could win him back. My hope was to eventually marry him and fulfill my hopes of having a unified household. I wanted the perfect all American household that society had been spoon feeding us since the beginning of time. How dare he deprive me of my dreams and make me another statistic!

Each time I would have high hopes of getting back together with my son's father but all I would get was my feelings hurt. It took me years to get over the failed relationship. My son's father and I were constantly arguing and at one another's throat- me because I was bitter and him; well I can't speak for him.

Well time heals all and eventually I did move past him. That chapter of my life was almost a decade ago and the fact is that regardless of our failed relationship, we still had a son to raise. We did in fact raise that son and he is now a man but it was not easy by any means! And it took a village to raise him! We had our son at the tender ages of 18 and 19 and the fact is that we were babies. It is very difficult to raise a child, simultaneously deal with a difficult parent and look past the feelings of hurt at the same time.

I have no regrets about having my first born at a young age. If it not for him I probably would have not been as grounded as I became. Prior to becoming pregnant with my son it was party central during the weekend and continuous class skipping during the week. I certainly could not have continued on that path and been successful in life.

Listen, you may not get along with your child's father but the reality of it is there is a very good chance that you knew what type of person he was before you decided to have sex with him.

You will continue to live your life and learn from your past mistakes with any new relationship that comes your way. Moving forward you must look at the red flags: Do not ignore the warning signs that people exhibit in the beginning of the relationship.

Like Chris Rock said, people show their representative in the beginning of the relationship. You do not know who the person truly is until you get to know them. On the flip side I have known people that have had decade long relationships only to wake up one day and find out they were sleeping with the enemy!

The bottom line is to watch a person's actions and their actions will tell you everything you need to know. People do not change unless they want to.

A word to the wise: You cannot keep a man by having a baby. I repeat, you cannot keep a man by having a baby! Don't expect a drastic turn of events just because you have had a child by this person. If you two get along then that is a plus. If you don't get along then you should work on building a relationship for the sake of your children. This is so important on so many fronts. A child needs to see that his parents are willing to do whatever it takes for his or her benefit.

Please remember that if you are no longer in a relationship with the father then this is not about you, but rather about your child. Sorry, put that pride to the side. We often don't consider how stressful it is for a child to have to deal with school, society, social issues and come home to deal with the drama of his parents. You may think he is not listening, but, oh, he is definitely listening! We don't give kids the credit they deserve. They are very smart and catch on fairly quickly when we think they don't. Kids are always, always watching and observing. So be careful.

One of my elders used to say: "Don't do what I do. Do what I say." Sounds good, and I am sure you have all heard this before. But usually kids will mimic exactly what you do and in the end we are left wondering why they chose the path they chose. Duh! They're looking at your actions.

And now I'm going to say what you surely don't want to hear: Someone has got to take the high road and unfortunately it may just be you. But you will thank yourself later, trust me. I spent so much time arguing with my son's father only for it to get me nowhere – a complete waste of time and energy.

Now don't get me wrong. You don't have to like one another but you do have to respect one another and you should try to the best of your ability to keep things civil. There may be times where negotiation is just not in the cards. If this is the case then you just may have to work things out through the court system. I hate when this happens but the court is designed to help parents work out amicable agreements for the benefit of the child.

Does going to court always work to your advantage? No, but at least it is an entity that may help. The sad reality is that we must all work with the cards that we have been dealt. We have to make the best out of a situation whether good or bad. Life goes on and so will you. No worries.

So we knew he was the person he was all along but we thought we could change him, right? Or we thought that having a baby would change him, right? Wrong! Stand in your truth and learn to separate reality from fantasy. My fantasy was to have the All-American family with my son's father but the reality of things was that it would never happen. I did not know how to "get out of my emotions". I was so blinded by love that I could not see the reality of the situation. The reality was that he had moved on emotionally from me but I had not done the same from him.

I know what I am telling you to do is easier said than done but it will be worth it in the end. Get a hobby, concentrate on your children. The best way to get past one situation is to throw your entire being into a new positive situation! You will be so busy you won't even have time to think about him. Yes, one day you will need to work through these feelings to ensure that you do not make the same mistake in future relationships. This does have to be today but eventually this is something that needs to be dissected and gotten to the bottom of.

Let me say this, it takes two to make a child no matter what the circumstances were when the baby was received. The man definitely needs to take care of his child and if you are unable to work something out you should by all means use your resources to enforce that right.

If the end result does not work in your favor then do not be bitter, be better: Do not hold it against the child. No matter what, the child still needs his or her father in their life if the father is willing to be there. If you and the father choose to stay together and can have a fruitful relationship, well then that's great, too!

The stigma

I, like many other females in the U.S., am considered a single mother, baby mama, baby moms or whatever else you wish to call it. The fact is, I am the mother of two children and I am unmarried.

Does that make me a bad person? Of course not. Does that mean my life is over as so many people will tell you once you become pregnant? No not at all. There are so many advantages to a child having both parents in the home but unfortunately not all mothers have that option. Does that mean we stop living? No, it just means that we adjust and keep it moving.

Life happens – I will repeat that again. Life happens! So you just roll with the punches. It is ideal to plan out your life and be proactive in providing a fruitful life for you and your family should you choose to have one. Now that I got that out of the way, let me say this: There are many single mothers that are minors.

By no means am I glorifying teenage pregnancy. At whatever age, a woman should make responsible decisions with her life and responsible sexual conduct is one of those decisions. It is always ideal to have some sort of structure in your life prior to bringing a life into this world. It just makes it easier for the child and for yourself to live a fruitful life. But, again, life happens. You need to make the most of any situation.

According to the U.S. Census Bureau, the number of child births to single women has increased since 1980, from 18.4 percent in 1980 to 40.6 percent in 2008 . The number of single-parent households has increased as well. In 1980, it was reported that 19.5 percent of households were single-parent households. That figure increased to 29.5 of households in 2008 (1).

At one point in society it was shameful and was looked down upon to be a single parent and be unmarried. Let's not pretend that it still did not happen, because the fact is that it did.

Never feel ashamed because you are a single parent. Your circumstances are your circumstances. It is funny how people always try to conform to the ways of society.

---

(1) HTTP://WWW.CENSUS.GOV/COMPENDIA/STATAB/2012/TABLES/12S1
337.PDF

Eons ago it was a sin to have a child out of wedlock and it was often looked down upon. Back in the day if you were to become pregnant and you were unmarried, you were sent down south to live with Aunt Lucy until the baby was born. Many times the baby was raised by another family member so that none were the wiser. It was not unusual to find out years later that 'Auntie' is actually your sister!

Why is it that once celebrities started adopting and having kids out of wedlock it became the thing to do? Now celebrities are having children out of wedlock every day. Some women or men are even adopting children now for several reasons such as not having the right mate in their lives, and they are not allowing society to shun them for wanting to give a child a loving home.

So, guess what? In 30 years it will be a different stigma for society to invent. I live for myself and don't conform to what people say is right. I create and carve out my own path in my life; as you can see. Don't get me wrong, being a single parent is not easy, ideally a two-parent household is very nurturing for several reasons, but it does not always work out like that and that is the reality.

Do not give up on your situation. You have to remain, spiritually, emotionally and physically adept in order to ensure that you are functioning for your children. Your children need you at your absolute best.

I have two children. The first child was born out of wedlock right after high school and the other child was born while I was married to my husband. Every time we make plans God laughs because he has something else in store for us.

The birth situation of my second child was much different. I was with my ex-husband for about 11 years. That was the longest relationship I had ever been in and as far as I was concerned I had not gotten married to get divorced.

What often happens is that a couple gets together at a very young age and one of two things happen: The couple either grows together or grows apart. Well, we grew apart and that's ok. We also grew to be very good friends and are still good friends till this day. He is a good father to our daughter and a great support system. This is a partnership that we have formed. I call it 'Partners in Parenting.'

I find it funny that many times outsiders will assume that because you not in a relationship with your child's father you both automatically have to be arch enemies. It is hilarious to coincidentally be at a party or event with my ex-husband and see the stares and glares of spectators. They are watching our body language to try and determine if we get along. I am glad that issue does not exist between us.

Even if there was drama, you would never know. Take note: Keep John and Jane Q. Public out of your business ladies and you will be better off. Besides people really don't care if you have drama with your children's father; they just want a show. Don't give them a show. People are drawn to drama.

We as women are so used to putting up with a man's bad behavior and letting it slide just because we want a man in our beds. Just to be able to say we are in a relationship. If he is exhibiting bad behaviors like lying, cheating, being cheap, not taking care of his children with other women, or not working, chances are that when you marry him or become pregnant with his child those behaviors will just intensify. People are who they are. They only change if and when they want to change. Don't waste your time and energy trying to change someone

Talk to women that have had the same experience as you about your situations, talk to one of the elders in your church or read a book on the topic. There is always knowledge to be gained by reading a book dedicated to the subject.

Don't be opposed to talking to a therapist or counselor about your problems. Many times an outside opinion from a non-biased person unfamiliar with the situation may be a good idea. Talking to a stranger may alleviate the fear of you being judged by your experiences. Check with your Human Resources Department to determine if there is an Employee Assistance Program (EAP) that may be able to assist you with free counseling.

Don't get me wrong, everyone has faults and no one is perfect but you have to decide within yourself if you want to live with this person and the characteristics that they display. If you think it is tolerable then by all means go ahead and have a relationship with this person. Or marry this man. But if you think that perhaps you cannot deal with the characteristics he's showing then perhaps you need to have a conversation with him and decide if you two will continue the relationship.

Moving on

Your children are here and now you must get on with your life and be the best parent that you can be for your children. This includes keeping your life straight, eating right, maintaining your health, and being diligent in regard to your finances.

I am not going to say that it will be easy moving on past the drama but it is the only way that you will regain your sanity. I read somewhere that the definition of insanity is doing the same thing over and over to only end up with the same result. It is like going in a never ending circle. You will eventually drive yourself insane by continuing in this downward spiral.

And one size does not fit all. I am by no means saying that my suggestions in this book are the end all, be all. You have to live your life and carve your path according to your destiny! You are the captain of your ship, take the wheel!

Life is about choices and in the words of the rapper T.I., make your next move your best move.

Go with your gut and you will know if you are making the right decisions in life. And guess what? Fall down 6 times, get up eight. Keep going. Be safe. Make a mistake? Get up and try it again until you get it right.

Many may judge you or even make fun of your journey. Yes they may even gossip about or hate on you but that is fine. People fear that which they will not take the time to understand. They wish they could get un-stuck. Many times people talk about others because they are envious of the moves the person is making and are scared to make changes in their own lives. Let them gossip standing still while you are maintaining and moving forward!

The Big 'D'

I know what you are thinking. Yeah the big 'D' the word called divorce. That I what you were thinking right?
No one want to talk about it but it is the big elephant in the room. Another way to become a single mom for sure is by being the product of a divorce.

Hopefully no one gets married with the intention of getting a divorce but the truth is that it happens. It happens in today's society more than we care to admit.

I once found myself on the other side of the big 'D' and it was a very confusing time for me. I went through a myriad of emotions immediately after I was divorced. I didn't know who to turn to and did not know what the future would hold for me. If someone would even mention the word marriage in my presence my whole demeanor would change.

I know that I needed help but I did not know where to turn. I turned to my friends and family. My friends and family were very supportive to me during this period of my life. It was a dark, dark period of uncertainty for me and if you have ever been depressed you know exactly what I'm talking about.

I was depressed and I knew that I had to do something about it. All I kept thinking was that this was the end of the line for me and that no one would ever love me again. I also knew that I was in bad shape and did not want my kids to see me in the depressed mood that I was in. I cried all the time, in the shower in the bed, in the car on the way to work. It was a sad time.

I remember my friend Linda coming over one day and telling me that I looked like hell. She told me that if I did not get to see a counselor or therapist within a week's time she was going to take matters into her own hand and force me into counseling!

Linda was right, something needed to be done and immediately. I was in bad shape. I was a zombie just walking through the motions of everyday life; work and then home to bed.

I didn't want to but I went to go see a counselor to work out the feelings that I was having. It was the best thing I could have ever done at that time in my life. There is such a stigma regarding counseling in the black community but the truth is that counseling can be very therapeutic.

With my counselor and my new plan to get my life on track I was on my way to the road to healing. It took me about a year but I was able to slowly get my life and mentality back on track.

I was very ashamed that my marriage had failed and that I was now a single mother of a very young infant and a teenage male. I was so embarrassed that I never even told my coworkers for several years that I was divorced. If they asked me about how my husband was doing I would make up a lie.

I eventually told them after I came to the realization that divorce does happen and that I would not be the first or last person to experience a divorce.

The Take-Aways:

o Be better not bitter

o You are better than your current situation

o Time marches on and so should you

o Make your next move your best move!

" God allows us to experience the low points in life in order to teach us lessons we could not learn in any other way. The way we learn those lesson is not to deny the feelings but to find the meanings underlying them." - Stanley Lindquist

CHAPTER 7
THE FACTS OF LIFE

Dating

Guess what? Just because I am a single mother does not mean I am dead! Nope, I am preserving my sexiness for the right man that comes along. I am only human and I am sure you feel the same. Just because you have children does not mean that you cannot date or have a boyfriend. But if you do you should exercise caution! You now have some little people to consider when you are determining whom to bring home. That is if he or she (yes she, everyone's lifestyle is different) is even worthy of introducing to your children.

For this reason, do not rush into introducing the person you are dating to your children. Dating is just a way of figuring out whether the person is a potential boyfriend. If you determine that the person is not a candidate for a potential relationship then no harm is done because you did not introduce him to your loved ones.

Yes, we single mothers need love, too, but we must also remember that our children did not ask to be here and should not suffer while we are off 'honey-dripping'. There should be no rush for a man to meet your children.

I once dated a guy that I worked with that waited an entire year to meet my kids while we dated. Yup! And once I was comfortable enough to let him know where I live he would pick me up outside my house and he knew he was not allowed in the house. Establish the rules straight out so that there is no confusion in the long run. In the words of one of my idols Wendy Williams, "Straight talk leads to straight understanding." If you tell someone what the situation is upfront there is no need for confusion on the back end — point blank.

You may decide that this man does not need to meet your child at all and that is fine also. I know women that have been in a relationship for years and waited a few years before they introduced their children to their mate. Find whatever works best for your situation.

Look, you are a grown woman and hopefully you use your best judgment in your dating life. It is a thin line between juggling a relationship and being the mother that your children need. So take your time in dating and find out if you have the time to date. The worst thing in the world is a mother that puts more energy into a man and dating while her kids suffer on the sideline. I have seen it a dozen times.

I once had a girlfriend that was so busy dating that she made no time for her child and had no idea what was going on in her daughter's school life. Every weekend she was dropping her daughter off to her parents while she 'did her'. It was a shock to her when she received a failing report card in the mail for her daughter. Go figure! If she had taken the time out to talk with her daughter and help her with her homework this is probably something that could have been prevented. In my opinion she was dead wrong in her actions! Ladies, make sure your priorities are straight. Never put a man above your kids.

As we get older the choices in the pool of available men get smaller and smaller. That does not at all mean that you should settle for the first man that comes along. Nor should you compromise your values. Women often settle for much more than they deserve and allow men to walk over top of them. Patience is key, God willing, you will find your soul mate.

Furthermore, stop looking in the same pond for the same fish. Open up your mind to dating men of other races, do a self-evaluation and determine if there is something about you that is blocking you from meeting your soul mate. Self-evaluation is always good for one to conduct on themselves from time to time. It is much easier to say than to do; believe me, I get it. I used to be one of those women that let a man run over them. I have had my share of heart ache from men. But if you know better, you do better. People can only do to you what you allow them to do to you. I now know better.

Just exercise caution in every situation because your children need you around. This includes safe sex. Yes, in the throes of passion all reasonable thinking goes out the window at times but you don't want to jeopardize you and your children's future for one night of passion. It's just not worth it. I don't know about you but I want to be around when my children's children have children if possible. Life is already short, you don't need a sexually transmitted disease to make it shorter or complicate a situation.

If he does not respect you enough to use protection then that is a red flag in and of itself and you should remove yourself from this situation immediately. At times we can let love blind us and cause us to make irrational decisions. In this case of dating think with your head and not your heart.

Finally, ladies we have to start valuing one another and stand as a united front with these men. We cannot allow or tolerate certain behavior.

The Man Code Deciphered

Sssshhh! I'm about to let you in on some secrets. The men are not going to like what I am about to say. We women don't understand that we hold the purse strings when it comes to relationships. We have it within our right to withhold 'it' for as long as we want. If a man is willing to wait instead of jumping in the bed with you that may speak volumes about his character.

I am not saying that because he waits to have sex with you that he is not dipping it low somewhere else. I am just saying that he may have a sincere interest in you. Time will determine if this is true.

There is the all famous debate regarding sex on the first night. I often hear on dating talk shows "Will he call me back if I sleep with him on the first night"? Well that depends on the man. I do not believe that this is a one size fits all answer for this question. Ask yourself what you are looking for out of this date? Are you looking for a one night stand or a lasting relationship? Your actions will determine the outcome of this situation.

Stand in your truth. Be honest with the person you are dating about what your expectations are. If you are looking for a relationship then let it be known. If you are looking for a friend with benefits then let it be known. Be careful what you ask for because you just might get it! Don't say you want a friend with benefits and then decide you want a relationship four months into the 'lustship'. Hopefully the person you are dating will be honest with you as well.

The truth about the matter is that no matter how honest you are with a person they may not reciprocate. For that reason many women will put up a wall and expect that the behavior from all men will be the same. This is not true. There are many men out there that are very honest in what they want and have no problem telling you exactly what it is that they want.

Don't be afraid to love again. If you are feeling it and the right vibes are there then go for it. Unfortunately you just have to put yourself out there even at the risk of getting hurt. If you keep a wall up how will prince charming get over the wall? And if you do get hurt, if it does not work out then that's ok. You will be fine over time and yes you will live!

Think with your head and weed out the bad apples right away. When men or people tell you who they are believe them. Watch their actions and not their words.

Remember, dating should be fun. When I was on the dating scene I always went out with the intention of having fun, not looking for my next husband.

After my divorce, I had plenty of fun with dating. I would meet the men I dated lots of places like online, parties, the grocery store or just walking down the street; you name it. You never know where and when you will run into Mr. Right; be prepared.

Keep an open mind. My ideal future mate in my mind was brown skinned and 6 foot 2. Wouldn't you know that the men that were approaching me never fit that description!

One day I had an 'ah-ha' moment. I realized the error of my ways. Suppose I had been missing out on my Mr. Right because he had not fit my desired description? Right then and there I decided to keep an open mind about dating.

Lastly, if you decide to date do not expect any expectations and go with the flow. They say that if you expect nothing than you will never be disappointed when nothing happens. Men can spell desperation a mile away and that may work against you. My male friends often tell me that there is nothing sexier than a confident woman. Walk in the room and command it! There is nothing sexier than a woman that exudes confidence and expresses exactly what she wants. Pull no punches ladies. Good luck.

Love yourself more

Do you love yourself? Of course you do that's a silly question right? Remember I said a few paragraphs ago to watch actions not words? Actions determine the truth I don't care what comes out of your mouth.

If you are letting any man into your bed and putting up with disrespectful behavior from him like: letting him live with you for free, taking care of him financially, letting him break your heart, constant lying, cheating, etc., then you do not love yourself I don't care what you say.

It gets lonely at night and the other side of that bed gets cold; oh so cold. Brrrrrrr. I know, I have been in the same position as you. I would give anything for a warm body in the bed across from me but at what price? Love yourself more to know that you deserve better than for your bedroom door to be a turnstile for any man. Right after my divorce I was literally a doormat for whomever wanted to whip his feet.

There are men out here, not all, that make it their business to prey upon the souls of weak women and break them down until they are nothing. The women become damaged and are no good to anyone not even her children. The man then moves on to the next unassuming victim.

If I can smell you from here than so can he. You stink! You are desperate and your bones are reeking from desperation and men like this can smell you from miles away. He may prey on you because of his own twisted issues that he himself has not dealt with.

I don't care how lonely you get ,stop falling for the okey-doke and what I call the 52-fake out; making a person assume something different than what the actual intention is. If a man is into you, you will know it. There will be no game playing he will upfront and honest about what he wants.

You deserve so much more than a 'wet back' and a broken soul just because you were lonely and looking for a warm body and thought that any body would do. Be patient and your time will come. In the interim work on you so that when your King arrives you will be ready to receive him. Make yourself happy instead of looking for someone else to make you happy. You should already be happy and when you finally meet Mr. Right he will only enhance your happiness.

Let me also say that a person can only do what you allow. Stop playing the victim all of the time ladies. You saw the red flags and you probably knew what this man was all about but you stayed so now it's his fault. He messed up and gave you excuses but you continued to tolerate his behavior time and time again. Yes, you played a part in this too. Bottom line is, you have to love yourself more!

Social networking

Social networking is great for many things: catching up with old schoolmates, locating lost ones, keeping in touch with friends and family. It's a great tool! But as much as it is a great concept it can also be your downfall if you let it. I often hear people state that social media breaks up what I call 'ships' - relationships, friendships and yes even lustships.

No, social networks do not break up 'ships', the use of these social networks by people are what break up 'ships'.

Just be careful on these networks. And remember, it is easy for a person to portray him or herself as someone they are not. You don't know these people! People lie and connive for their own selfish reasons. Why? I cannot tell you nor should you or I try to figure out why. Just know that you need to be careful of what you are posting on these public networks.

If it is written on Facebook or Twitter or, yes, even Instagram, it cannot ever totally be erased permanently. Yes there are privacy options on these networks but even those are not a guarantee that information about you will not be leaked on the internet.

There is also the topic of the almighty search engine Google. In this day and age you can plop anyone's name in that Google browser bar and come up with just about any and all information and pictures about the person. The bottom line is that information posted on the internet can be pulled up at a later time if need be. Nothing ever fully disappears, nothing.

I have friend that learned a valuable lesson about posting information on a social network. This friend was known for posting racy jokes and pictures on his Facebook page. In his eyes, his actions may have been innocent; I mean he was not hurting anyone and he was just having a great time by posting things to make his friend laugh. I mean I even found some of his posts hilarious.

Unfortunately, his current employer was not amused. Some of the posts were discovered by the Human Resources Department and he was terminated from the company. In the eyes of the company the character that he displayed on the internet was not in line with the expected behavior of employees. A valuable lesson was learned here at the expense of job loss. I sure hope it was worth it. Many jobs these days are requiring that employees sign a clause that prohibits certain behavior on the internet and social networking sites.

I have had many experiences in which I have met people on social media and became friends with them. In the end they turned out to be other than what they represented themselves to be on social networks. All I can say is that it is fine to befriend people but just be careful!

Use your best judgment when interacting with people on these networks. And be cautious whom you are letting view your valuable pictures and information.

I see people make an announcement on social media that they are going on vacation. The next thing they know they have been robbed! Yes, there are privacy settings but can anyone say they are guaranteed? Just exercise caution when interacting on these networks.

As I've stated in previous chapters: Many times we see the red flags but we ignore them, we hear the little voice in our head telling us that something is not right, yet we still continue down the same path. Your instincts will never steer you wrong. Listen to them and take notes!

I'm not trying to attack social media because it can be positive on many different levels, but don't let it take over your life and hinder you from your everyday activities such as spending time with your kids and taking time out to spend with yourself.

I actually was able to reconnect with some long last family members as a result of being on social networks. If it were not for the internet, many things may not be possible in this fast paced world.

I grew up and currently still live along the Jersey Shore. During Hurricane Sandy in October of 2012 there were wide spread power outages in most of New Jersey and the Tri-state area. This may have been possibly the biggest natural disaster within my memory while living in New Jersey.

Many New Jersey Residents went without power for at least five through ten days while the utility companies scrambled to try and restore electricity to New Jersey Citizens. At the time my children were 18 and 5 years of age. It was one of the most difficult experiences in my life but I was blessed to be able to provide for our needs and my house was still standing after the storm passed. Many friends were not so lucky and are still to this day trying to piece their lives together.

In the area that I live in New Jersey, we had never really experienced power loss so when we lost power (and heat) for five days straight I thought I would lose my mind. Imagine how hard it was to keep a five year old entertained in the dark. Needless to say my son and I got very creative!

I really should not complain, because others in the Tri-State area faired far worse than me. I knew families that had lost entire homes and belongings as a result of the storms. That was one of my most humbling experiences as of my adult life. There were no guarantees for anything. No guarantee of when the electric would be back on, no guarantee of when the store shelves would be stocked with food again, no guarantee of when the water in my basement would recede. One of the only things that was guaranteed was that there was a God. There was also social media and the internet was still up and running thus providing a communication port to the open world.

My social network friends and I used the internet and social media to keep one another abreast of all current events happening during this horrible storm. If it were not for social networks, I do not know how I would have made it through. That is one blessing that I was grateful for during that time of disaster. For as much drama that happens on social networks that was one time that everyone stood together and showed a united front. It was invigorating!

Don't worry, two weeks later it was back to the usually banter. What happen to the unity?

I say all this to say, use these types of outlets in moderation but use them to your advantage. Don't read into too much that is posted on these social sites. If you find yourself consumed with social media then perhaps it is time to take a step back and reevaluate what you are using the medium for. That is all that I will say about that.

Social media has been bad for me but it has also done a lot of good! For instance if it were not for social media I would never have met the acquaintance of some of the fantastic people that are in my life now life like Faith, Jennifer and a slew of other interesting people. It has also helped me promote the release of this book and brings awareness of the good I am doing through my organization Single Moms Rock! So I use social media for what it's worth. I don't sweat the small stuff, after all it's just small stuff!

Friends, how many of us have them?

As I have gotten older, I have learned that true friends come a dime a dozen. You may have several associates but how many do you really, actually, truly know that you can call a tried and true friend? As you get older you notice that your circle of friends may get smaller and smaller and that is OK. Friends outgrow one another sometimes. The same interests you shared when you were younger may not be the same interests you share today.

People have kids, become engaged or even married. People tend to hang around others that share the same interests; women with small children may seem to gravitate toward other women with small children and such.

Not to make you paranoid about people but you need to watch who newly meet and befriend. Not all but some people have agendas or want to use you for their own benefit and then when they are finished drop you off like a kid at a pool. Not every person is out to get you but just be careful of who you tell your innermost secrets. Let them earn that right to come into your world and know what makes you tick.

Remember if they gossip to you, they will gossip about you! There is nothing worse than sharing a secret with a person and that person running off and starting a telephone line of the story you told. The next thing you know the story has been changed 20 times by the time it gets back to you ----- and it will eventually get back to you. Save yourself the time and embarrassment of being hurt by gossip.

I will never forget a young lady that I met on social network that was nothing but a conniver. She was only interested in her own interests. She was so sweet initially but her true colors eventually shined through. She would sit with me and converse about people that were supposedly her best friends. She would tell me their inner most secrets. So why would I be surprised with some of the personal things I told her about me came full circle back to me? At first I was shocked and could not believe that this could happen to me. But the reality of the situation is that I did not look at the red flags. Had I looked at the red flags I would have saw the type of person she was and the character that she possessed.

You live and you learn. And I learned a hard lesson here. Good thing for me, I had not told this girl any of my true innermost secrets. Again, when someone shows you who they are, believe them! It's ok to be friendly with people, but just be cautious and protect your interests. Not everyone needs to know your deepest and darkest secrets some things should remain with you and be taken to the grave.

Only share what you would feel comfortable with if it were to be printed on the front page of the newspaper, at least that's what they used to say back in the day. In this day and age, only tell what you would feel comfortable telling if it were put in a Facebook status or blasted on Twitter!

I can't say enough "When people show you who they are, believe them." In other words, if someone is showing you that they are a gossip why would you trust them with your most precious secrets? What would stop them from turning on you and telling the world your secrets?

If someone lies on their income tax , tries to defraud the government from money, is deceptive in nature then why would they keep it real and be honest with you all the way around? What makes you so special? Who are you? Exactly – if they can't keep it real with themselves then why should they keep it real with you?

If an individual is always caught up in drama and always caught in drama with others then something may be wrong with that person and you need to run, not walk, away. Everyone can't always be wrong! Just saying! The person may appear to play the victim but look closely.

Usually if we think back to a bad friendship we realize that there were signs along that way that we just ignored. The red lights were glaring and the sirens were going off but we chose to ignore them. Just like the person in the horror films walking through the forest when they hear a rustling – instead of investigating they keep walking through the woods. Lada dee lada dah…..next thing you know the killer is right in front of them but they ignored the red flags tipping them off that something wasn't right. Proceed with caution.

As I am getting older, my circle of friends is getting smaller and smaller. At first I was upset about this and wondered if it was that my friends didn't love me anymore or that they just did not want to make time for me. But the reality is that people are living their lives and have much more responsibilities than they did when we were younger… Life is busy.

I would often become upset when I would reach out to friends and try to keep in touch but the feeling was not reciprocated. I am a person that does not take rejection well and it would hurt at times. But then one day I woke up and reminded myself that friendship is not a one way street. A friendship is a form of a relationship and it takes two to make it work.

When I love, I love hard! I am very territorial about the people that I truly care about. I hold people to a high standard and when they fail to meet that standard I become upset. I have to realize that people fall short but it's not their fault. It is just who they are as a person and there is nothing wrong with that.

Or perhaps the person just does not consider you as important in their life anymore. I never fault people for their feelings. Point blank, if the other person is not meeting you half way then you are wasting your time and energy. Have a talk with the person and let them know how you feel. If nothing changes then take your heart and move on.

So guess what? Choose quality over quantity. If you have a few good friends then you are all the better off in life. If you are the type of person with no friends that is fine too, be friends with the Lord or be friends with yourself.

On the flip side of the coin, as we get older responsibilities increase with jobs and family, significant others, etc. Just don't forget your true friends and understand that the telephone works both ways. If you have not heard from a friend in a while, pick up the phone and give him or her a call. Invite them out for coffee or dinner. Just move on with your life and don't hold grudges. Life is too short.

I am blessed to have known my closest friends Tiffany, Quiche and Arlicia since grade school. Tiffany is my bestie and also the Godmother of my daughter and has always, always been there for me. We both lead busy lives but when we get together, we pick right back up where we left off. Quiche and Arlicia are like close sisters and are always available when I need them. Above all I value the friendship of these ladies and hope we remain as close in the years to come.

Mentors and Role Models

Who in life do you look up to? Everyone should have a role model, mentor or someone they look up to, one that you really look up to for the right reasons. It is nice to look up to people in the celebrity world; as a lot of people do, but keep a person in mind that is tangible. Someone that you can actually reach out and touch and have a serious discussion with.

I for one enjoy having conversations with my elders. They have a story to tell and nine times out of ten they have experienced a lot more in life than we have. It's better to talk to someone that has been through it, right? For instance, why take marriage tips from someone that has never been married? Does that make sense to you? Stop getting advice from your bitter girlfriends that have never had a lasting and positive relationship with a man and therefore cannot lend advice.

My role model is my mother; she was the backbone of our household. She lost her own mother at a very young age but still was able to do well in life. She has always worked hard her entire life and has introduced her children to things in life to ensure they were well-rounded. And guess what? I find myself doing the same thing as a mother. We were not rich but lower middle class. We grew up in a house and basically led a happy childhood for the most part.

It was common for us to vacation every summer and visit museums in New York City. My mom managed to save money each year so that we could make excursions like this. If there were troubles in the home, we were unaware as kids. My mom shielded us from events that we would later find out about as adults. Now that I am older I can appreciate her more and I hope that my children will have the same appreciation for me in later years.

All while raising kids my mom was able to become a Registered Nurse and later return to school to obtain an MBA after the age of 50. It was intimidating for her to return to school after so many years but she stayed encouraged and accomplished that feat.

We were actually able to graduate together from Monmouth University in May 2006 and that I will never forget that day. We may have made history as the first mother-daughter duo to graduate from the college on the same day. The local paper actually came out and wrote a feature story on us both. That was one of the best experiences of my life. I only hope to be as strong of a woman as my mother is.

I also look up to a woman that I will call "Mrs. A". I love her dearly and as they say: "Mother has lived". We initially crossed paths after I applied for a job at her clothing store. I was a young single mother looking for a flexible part time job and she provided me the opportunity to work in her store.

That was more than seventeen years ago and since that time Mrs. A has been on the sidelines as I have developed into the young successful woman that I am today. She saw me struggle as a single parent of a 2-year-old and move up the ranks. I have valued her advice over the years and came to her many times for advice. She has been very successful in her career and has raised three very successful beautiful daughters as well. I am considered her fourth daughter; in my eyes anyway. Why would I not take her advice? Oh, how I love visiting her house and sitting in the kitchen on a stool while she cooks a meal for us and reminisces about the days of old.

The Lord brought her into my life for a reason, especially at a time when I needed her the most. There is a reason and a season for everything.

In short, find someone to talk to that you respect and admire. People are usually willing to help a person that is honestly trying to do well in life. It is called paying it forward. Once you found that you have made it to the point where you are satisfied with your life, lean back and pull someone else up by the boot straps.

The Take-Aways:

o Dating should be fun!

o We hold the purse strings ladies

o Be careful who you call a friend!

o Use social networking for what it is worth

o It is important to have a mentor

My loves!

"When you've given all you got, and you got nothing left to give, then focus on the road ahead, and just stay positive." – Author unknown

CHAPTER 8
THE ROAD AHEAD

If you wake up every morning with the attitude that you hate life, guess what? Life will absolutely, positively hate you right back! Attitude determines altitude! If you put out positive vibes in the environment they will come back to you tenfold. Trust me on this one. No, every day won't be sunshine and birds singing sweet melodies but that doesn't mean you can't learn from it! Take each day one day at a time. Don't rush through life!

I remember in my younger years I used to be so stressed out about everything! Any little thing that did not go according to plan would cause me to stress out to a level like no other. After years of stressing out about things that I could not change I wound up with high blood pressure. Yes, I am convinced that the years of stress finally caught up to me. And many times when we stress out it is about situations that are minute in nature or about things that we do not have the power to change.

So guess what? If you are not in the position to change something, then change the way you think about it.

As the kids always say: YOLO. You Only Live Once. Sure, it's a catchy tune that the rapper Drake has made a rap song out of; but it is so true! Life is too short to do anything else but enjoy it. I have seen people drop dead at young ages and it is a terrible thing. So, take it slow and take the time to smell the roses. It will give you a better appreciation of life and present you with another way to handle the situations you are facing. Always remember that cooler heads prevail.

I would be remiss if I did not end the book and dedicate a chapter to the bright future ahead. After we are done playing superwoman and taking care of the kids, job, home and others, it's time to take care of Mom! Yes, you need to find the time to regroup so that you can continue to be the extraordinary woman that you are.

I know what you are going to say: "But I never find the time." Well, make the time! People find time for what they want, so find some way to have some "me" time each week. Start off on a small scale, after household chores and getting the kiddies into bed. Take some time to read a book, watch television or write in a journal. This can be not only satisfying but a healthy practice to clear your head after a trying day as well.

Doctor's always tell us that humans require a good night's sleep of at least eight hours. A solid investment of a good night's sleep is worth the sacrifice so that you can conquer the next day and eventually the week ahead of you.

Once you find the time on a daily basis to have some quality time with yourself, try graduating to larger amounts of time, like Sunday afternoon while the kids are on a play date or with their dad or a relative.

If you can never get away here are some other alternatives: Meet up with a mom you trust and take turns watching each other's kids while the other takes a break or gets errands done. If you work and are able to take time off, take what I call a mental health day. Take some time off from work to regroup while the kids are in school or daycare. Just find the time somewhere!

Come up with a nightly ritual to get yourself ready to wind down for the night. There are little things you can do, like giving yourself a manicure and pedicure while listening to your favorite CD. Running a bubble bath and getting some candles from the dollar store and placing them around the tub. Make yourself a cup of chamomile tea and there you have it! So relaxing to sit in a bathtub and soak while sipping on a cup of tea! But be careful with those candles, we don't want a fire. Always exercise caution.

Once you are able there are other little things that you can do to help you relax and get back to you. I use my "me time" every Sunday while my daughter spends time with her dad. I dedicate the entire day to myself and do things like have breakfast by myself at my favorite breakfast nook, go for a walk on the beach, carry my journal with me and jot down thoughts, or at times I even schedule a personal massage at least once every other month. I love it, it gives me a chance to take a deep breath and get ready for the busy week ahead.

Whether I lay in the bed, go shopping, get my nails done or go out on a date with my honey, the point is I have no kids to worry about and I get to let down my hair and kick my feet up! Be creative and find time for 'you'! Work it out!

Live your life for you

Remember, you are living your life for you and not anyone else. You have chosen to make the choices in your life. Now you must live with the circumstances, whatever they may be. When you live your life the way someone wants you to live it then, guess what? You are not living your life, you are living their life.

At the risk of sounding like a know-it-all, I have always skipped to my own beat. Many people told me to quit school and get a full-time job to take care of my son. I did not listen and continued to go to school and work part-time to support my son. Did we sacrifice for a few years? Yes, but it was all worth it. I was creative and still able to be there for my son, to provide quality time and keep a roof over our heads.

If I would have listened to those people I would never have made it as far as I made it today. I love living life on the edge and taking risks but, hey, that's just me. I'm not encouraging anyone to be like me, but you have to make your own decisions in life. Always go with your gut; it will never steer you wrong. It's just important to make wise decisions.

There was a time as an adult that I looked for approval from everyone and tried to be a people-pleaser. I did that for many years. I was not happy during that time but I was always looking for approval from others in order to feel validated. I was also very shy at one point and would barely speak upon walking into a room. Guess what this behavior got me: ran over, looked past, disrespected. You get the point so I won't continue. This behavior basically got me nowhere. If you are living your life according to the way that another person expects you to live life, you are not living your life; you are living their life!

The good thing about life is that you live and learn from past experiences. I learned quickly as I moved into my 30s that I better open up my mouth and start living for Kei or I would never get out of this funk. I am such a different person today than I was 20 years ago and I think that is true for most people. It just means that I am growing as a woman and just getting better with age!

Now it is difficult for me to even keep my mouth closed. I am definitely more assertive in nature at work and in my personal life. Don't get me wrong, I am still a sweetheart but don't ever take my kindness for weakness.

24 Hour Pity Party

Ok, I get it. Every day is not going to be a sunny day and it may rain but that does not mean that you cannot dance in the rain. Every day you wake up you will not have a positive attitude regarding some things; you just won't and that is the reality of things. I am all about living in my truth and keeping it real about my situation and so should you.

Therefore, on the bad days I am allowing you 24 hours to just sit and have a pity party. All day just sit in your 'crap' as they say. Sit all day long and cry, ponder and reflect on the incident and try and determine what you could have done differently. The only rule to this pity party is that the next day you need to lift yourself up and continue on your journey and no longer dwell on what went wrong. You need to never go back to that bad place again. Cry, scream in an empty room, jump up and down, go to the kick boxing class at your gym but you have 24 hours to get this negative energy out. Negative energy stored is like a time bomb waiting to explode. What a bomb explodes it is difficult to pick up the pieces and rebuild what was destroyed. Now let's go!

Life Happens

They always say when one door closes five more open. I truly believe this. There have been so many doors shut in my face, from mortgage companies to employment, to being laid off from work in 2011. Yet, being let go from my company was the best thing that could have happened to me. The day they handed me paperwork and told me my last day in the office would be June 11, 2011, I just stared at the paperwork and smiled. I knew, that there were bigger and better things out there for me.

There were several hundred employees let go that day. When my coworkers found out I was one of those several hundred persons laid off, they scrambled to my desk and with the assumption that I was upset by the news only to find me smiling from ear to ear. They were confused and thought they would find a different reaction to the news. I wasn't worried, I was overjoyed because I knew I had wanted to make an exit but I was just awaiting a sign from God that it was ok to move on. Sure enough I found a job 6 months later at which I am still employed.

There were some devastating things that happened to me along the way in this journey where I felt like I would never make it through, but I did. I kept the faith somehow, some way.

You just need to take one day at a time. No matter how you plan, there will always be some glitch or wrench that gets thrown in the plan. That's life. You have to roll with the punches and continue on, no matter how hard it gets.

I have to say that my journey has not been easy by any means. I had a rough life but I would not change a thing about it. Your experiences shape you into the person that you will become. Yes, there were bad and good experiences and I even learned from the bad experiences. Just because an experience was bad does not mean that you cannot learn from it.

One day I woke up and decided that I was blessed and that I, in turn, should share some of my blessings with others so that they may benefit. Sort of like a pay-it-forward type of deal. People always say that you are better off once you determine your purpose on this earth and God's reason for putting you here. In other words, we should all be living a purpose-driven life.

I believe my purpose on this earth is to help single mothers, so that they do not suffer through the same plight as I did when I first started out raising my son alone.

I know what you are saying. Now that I have read this book, where is the author now? What is she doing with her life? Well as I approach my 39th birthday I must say that I am the best that I have ever been in my entire life. As I have gotten older I have gotten better. I have two wonderful kids, I am successful in life and I am living the life that I dreamed about as a young child.

I also now have a very supportive man in my life whom I adore and who has taught me how a lady should be treated. He is nothing but a true gentleman, is caring and treats me like the queen I am.

I am working in the industry and a job that I absolutely love. The company and the people that I work for are great. Hopefully I will retire from this company.

I am also continuing to take time to stop and smell the flowers. I have learned from my past mistakes and moving forward in hopes not to make those mistakes again. I am also learning to cherish friendships and family because life is too short.

I think the hardest point of my journey has been continuing to stay on track financially and keeping control of my health. What can I say I am a work in progress and it is a something that I work on daily. I advise you to do the same. I am by no means perfect, but if I find something that I am not good at I keep working at it until I get it right.

I am just like you. I come from humble beginnings. I remember my first apartment starting out on my own was full of roaches and the occasional run through of a mouse. I am not very fond of cats but I remember buying a cat in hopes of keeping the mice away. Oh the good ole days!

I remember laying in my bed awake at night and saying to myself that this was only temporary. Bigger and better things were on the horizon for me. I remember being a boarder in a rooming house with my first child because I could not afford to pay daycare plus the cost of an apartment.

I also remember being evicted countless times from apartments because I could not afford to pay the rent and moving back home. I remember me having to move from those apartments and leaving with just my clothes because I did not have anywhere to put my furniture. My expenses were far more than the income I was receiving each month. I remember a lot of things about the early days. I also know that I am never too humble or good to work at a fast food restaurant or scrub floors in order to feed my family. I am not above that.

I am a survivor and a hustler. It is in my blood. My father has always worked for himself. He is a self-made entrepreneur. He is by no means rich but no one ever handed him anything. He also comes from humble beginnings from growing up in the deep south.. He has always worked for himself. He once told me that as long as a man has a truck he can make a dollar! And I truly believe that.

I say all this to say don't give up on your situation. If I can do it than so can you. It will not happen overnight but it will happen. With a strong will and determination anything is possible. And when you have made it, pay it forward. Extend a hand and help the next person up.

As I wrote this book it was my hope to inspire single mothers everywhere. I know the road is hard because I have been there. I lived and worked in the worst places so

I am just giving you an honest account of what I have been through on this long journey. I cried to myself at night and prayed that things would get better after time with my situation.

Then I just started taking one day at a time, putting one foot in front of the other to try and make it work. And eventually it did.

At times it breaks my heart to see a young girl pushing a baby that looks herself to be a baby, but I remember that that was once me. I cannot save the world, but if my story can encourage one woman or can give one woman hope on her journey then I will take that. I have helped one person and hopefully that woman will pull someone else up by the bootstraps and help her along the way. Always treat another woman how you would want them treated if she were your mom, or your aunt or daughter. I will end by saying - All the best my friend, good luck on your new journey; the rest of your life starts now.

Are you ready?

Me and the Kiddies!

More Food For Thought

- ❖ People will make time, for what they want to make time for.

- ❖ Life is too short!

- ❖ You can't control others actions, but you can control your reaction.

- ❖ It's not the number of times you get knocked down that matters; it's how many times you get back up.

- ❖ When a person tells you (show) who they are, believe them!

- ❖ What Sally says about Jane, says more about Sally

- ❖ Knowledge is Power

I say this often

SERENITY PRAYER

God grant me the serenity

to accept the things

I cannot change.

The courage

to change the things I can,

and the wisdom

to know the difference.

These are a few of my favorite things..........

Resources for Single Moms

www.yessinglemomsrock.com

www.cafemom.com

Free stuff!

www.calendarforkids.com

Finance

www.thebudgetnista.com

www.suzeorman.com

www.DaveRamsey.com

www.annualcreditreport.com

Education

www.thesinglemothers.com

www.fafsa.ed.gov

Weight/Health Management

www.myfitnesspal.com

Careers

www.Linkedin.com

www.Monster.com

www.Indeed.com

ABOUT THE AUTHOR

Kei Renae resides in central New Jersey and holds an undergraduate degree in Business from Monmouth University, Long Branch, New Jersey and an MBA from Devry's Keller Graduate School. Renae is also a Senior Project Manager at a major fortune 500 Healthcare Company. Renae is the mother of two children ages 5 and

19 and beloved dog GiGi and is also the founder of an organization called 'Single Moms Rock!" (SMR).

SMR! is dedicated to the empowerment of single mothers.

Please review the website for information at

www.yessinglemomsrock.com.

For speaking engagements please contact Kei at:

info@yessinglemomsrock.com.

www.yessinglemomsrock.com